Team Honey Badger

Raising Fearless Kids in a Cowardly World

Team Honey Badger:
Raising Fearless Kids in a Cowardly World

Paul G. Markel
Copyright 2015
All Rights Reserved

Dedication

This book is lovingly dedicated to my three honey badgers; Jarrad, Paxton, and Zachary. Though they are grown and capable of acting as sheepdogs, I trust that they will take the lessons they have learned and embrace them, while keeping their badger spirit alive in whatever situation they may find themselves.

For my grandchildren yet unborn; I pray this book will be a way to preserve the lessons and ideals that should be passed down to them.

Paul G. Markel August 18, 2015

Team Honey Badger

Raising Fearless Kids in a Cowardly World

Foreword

Every generation owes it to the successive one to pass on the lessons they have learned. Mankind has understood this concept for thousands of years. Our forefathers realized the value of understanding history and of continued education. The founding fathers of the United States of America were intimately familiar with human history and the lessons learned by the previous generations of men.

The original documents used to govern the nation were not simply made up on the spot. They were based upon hard fought and hard learned lessons of men and their governments throughout time. The founding fathers understood the value of education and considered it to be the duty of every citizen to ensure that the lessons of history and human interactions be passed on to their posterity.

Here, in the great enlightened era of the 21st Century, we have a dangerous situation playing out. The current youth generation, and for a large part the one that preceded it, have a woeful lack of understanding of human history and the history of interactions amongst men.

From my perspective, there are two primary causes for this lack of education and understanding. The first one is the most insidious while the second reason is more a byproduct of a cultural change due to technological advancement.

Political Correctness, or the desire to appease every person regardless of the subject at hand, has been ongoing for at least twenty years in earnest. The most dangerous or insidious thing about the PC culture is that it has established a strong foothold in all levels of primary and secondary schooling. History lessons are shortened, removed, or altered in the interest of being politically correct. Facts are replaced by teachers' opinions. Lessons that our grandparents knew and understood are completely lost on the current generation as they have been glossed over or eliminated completely so as not to offend someone somewhere.

The second reason I believe that today's young people are so ignorant of the history of human interaction is due to the "Information Superhighway." With information about most any topic or subject available with a few short keystrokes or button taps, the adult generation has gotten intellectually lazy. Modern adults do not take the time to pass on history lessons to their young people. "Kids today are so much more advanced than we were." is a lame and empty cop out offered by lazy adults.

To the previous statement I say "Horse-hockey!" The ability to push buttons and play with shiny new gadgets does not denote intelligence. The current youth generation is comprised of glittering jewels of colossal ignorance. (credit to Rush Limbaugh) Plainly put, these young skulls full of mush do not know what they do not know, but they have been convinced that their opinion on every matter is critically important.

It is time for every responsible adult member of society to do two things. First, reject political correctness as the cultural poison that it is. Fight PC jerks at every turn and point out the folly of their ways. Secondly, stop expecting the Internet to educate your children. Just because the information is available at the tip of their fingers does not mean that they will either see it or comprehend it. Yes, I am asking you to work harder and dedicate yourself to the fight, but what is your other option? Continue on the current path and watch as the nation crumbles.

As I have advised in previous books, grab a pen, pencil and/or a highlighter. Take notes in the margins and leave reminders for yourself. A well-worn, highlighted and penciled book is a compliment to any author.

Also, be a man (or a woman), brew a fresh pot of premium coffee and light a hand rolled Dominican if you have access to one. Live like a free person.

-PGM

Introduction

The gun culture loves to use the terms "sheep, wolves, and sheepdogs." Naturally, responsible gun owners like to consider themselves to be the sheepdogs of the world, keeping watch over society's sheep. Animal references are nothing new. Going back to the Old Testament and then the New, you will find the mention of people being like goats and sheep or brave and courageous like lions. Evil men are referred to as jackals and wolves. Deceitful men are serpents or snakes.

Animal kingdom references will likely be popular for the entirety of human existence. We ascribe feelings, emotions, and attributes to certain animals. Brave as a lion. Sly as a fox. Loyal as a dog. Stubborn as a mule.

Keeping with our discussion of the gun culture, you and I might refer to ourselves as sheep dogs, but does that also apply to our children? Perhaps your sons and daughters might grow up to be adults and sheep dogs in their own right, but what about when they are young? When my daughter was 11 years old I would not have said she was a sheep dog, even though she knew how to use a gun and was very mature for her age. Is it the task of your school aged kids to be the "protectors of the flock?"

I have my son Zachary to thank for introducing me to the modern phenomenon of the honey badger. A National Geographic special about the life of the honey badger spawned a hundred knock-offs and the entire idea took off and became mainstream, even viral, if you will. The "Honey Badger Don't Give a Sh*t" video has been viewed millions upon millions of times and is quite a piece of entertaining material for big boys and girls.

All joking aside though, the wild honey badger has been listed by the Guinness Book of World Records as the "World's Most Fearless Creature." At first glance the honey badger seems like a cute and furry little animal, the kind you would expect to see in a Disney cartoon alongside a bunny and squirrel. Honey Badgers (HBs) are not imposing creatures. Their bodies are squat and they sit low to the ground. Adults honey badgers will weigh only 20 to 35 pounds.

The HB's mild appearance belies their sharp teeth and strong jaws; jaws that are strong enough to break a turtle shell. Their long claws aid in both digging and fighting. Covered with a loose skin, according to the Guinness Book "there is no safe place to hold" a honey badger as it can always maneuver itself to fight back. Honey badgers are omnivorous and consume meat and fruit. Essentially, HB eats most anything it darn well pleases.

Wildlife biographers and videographers have witnessed HB in the wild driving off lions and hyenas. HB eats, as one of the main parts of its diet, deadly snakes, such as the cobra and puff adder. HB is highly resistant to snake venom and a single bite that could kill the average human simply makes HB sleepy. The "honey" part of the name comes from the fact that HB likes to raid beehives to eat larvae and honey. Even hundreds of bees trying their best to sting HB does not dissuade him or her from the goal of fresh beeswax and larvae.

Finally, HB lives in some of the most inhospitable places on earth and still thrives. HB lives in the Kalahari Desert on the continent of Africa amongst some of the most dangerous predators in the world. Predators know to keep their distance from HB or very quickly learn the error of their ways.

If I could grant my children the characteristics of one animal on planet Earth, it would not be the sheepdog, it would be the honey badger. As we progress throughout this text we will consider ways that we can indeed instill the fearlessness of the honey badger in our children or grand-children from both a physical and psychological aspect.

Why not Longer?

Some of you might have purchased this manuscript and thought, "Why isn't it longer?" Well, Junior High remarks aside, the truth is I said what I thought needed to be said in the time allotted.

Many years ago, when I was starting out as a writer, an editor told me, "Make your point and then shut up." I was turning in 2500 word articles when he would have rather had 1500 words. I mistakenly thought that the more words, the better. Instead, he did not want to wade through and cut out all the unnecessary verbiage to fit the page space.

That same editor advised me that when I submitted articles to him he wanted 1500 to 1800 words maximum. "Anything else is just puking on the reader." he put so very eloquently. I learned to make my point and then shut up.

If you have purchased and read many parenting or child development books they can be several inches thick. I suppose if I took another year to write this I could fill it with anecdotes and childhood tales, but this book needs to be out and available now, not in 12 months.

And so, with that said, I trust that you will appreciate the quality of that which is presented herein, not simply the quantity. I like to think that we are all friends here, I would not puke on you deliberately.

Chapter 1

Strengthening the Fearless Mind

Our friend the honey badger (HB) is not the most "fearless creature" due to its size or strength. There are innumerable other animals that are larger, stronger, and faster than HB, yet it scares off and defeats foes that would put other animals on the run. The greatest attribute of HB is the fearless attitude that it embraces. Claws and teeth important, but they are worth nothing without the proper attitude to back them up.

Honey badgers possess a supreme intelligence in the animal kingdom. Those seeking to keep HB penned up for observation have a difficult time, as they are such excellent problem solvers. Honey badgers have been known to figure out how to unlatch a gate or use objects in their enclosure to build a bridge or ladder to climb out. They will burrow under a wall or fence and exploit any weakness in their cage or enclosure. Honey badgers have gotten into houses and opened the refrigerator and the drawers inside to feast on people food.

When considering teaching and training our children to be human examples of HB, the first place we should begin is with a fearless mind. More aptly, we must consider how We can help our kids to develop a fearless mind. After all, developing a fearless mind does not simply happen all by itself.

I believe we can all agree that a small child, infant or toddler, is much like an empty sponge. From the moment they enter the world they begin to take in and store memories, sensations, stimulations, and information. Infants learn the touch, sound, and smell of their mothers.

Their mother's voice and warm embrace are instantly equated with safety and comfort.

When they achieve mobility, crawling and then walking, the child sets out to test the world around it. Think about it. How many times can you remember your baby testing the consistency of gravity? Toddlers get into everything. They are testing and exploring their world, they are filling their fresh, fertile minds with experiences and stimulation. Toddlers are naturally fearless. They do not fear the stairs, the family dog, the wall socket. They have no fear of grabbing ahold of the tablecloth or any other object they can get their hands on.

As soon as your little one can understand the words coming out of your mouth you begin to teach them about what they should respect or fear. When we see them going for the wall socket we tap their hand and say "No." We teach them to respect fire, gravity and sharp objects as they grow. The stove is hot. Kitchen knives are not toys, etc. This education does not cause an irrational and irreversible fear of fire or knives or electricity. Children should learn a healthy respect for the dangers those things present. "Look both ways before crossing the street." That education does not create a paranoia about cars, but a conscious realization that getting hit by a moving car is a very bad thing.

It never ceases to amaze me that adults will breed hoplophobia (irrational fear of guns) into their children regarding firearms. "I can't have guns in my home, I have children" is a favorite quote from well-meaning and uneducated pseudo-adults. My response to that has always been, "Did you teach your kids not to play with matches, to look both ways before crossing the street, not to stick a fork in the wall socket?" You did? Then why can't they be taught that guns are not toys and we do not play with them?

Every year in the United States of America children die from falls, poisoning, burns, car crashes, and drowning, yet we still allow them to ride in cars. We have ant poison and bleach in our homes. We have a stove and a bath tub. We even have gravity in and around our house. Do we dress our kids in bubble wrap suits with hockey helmets and face shields and make them wear rubber gloves? Of course not. We educate them and give them the information they need to mitigate risk and make good decisions.

There is a movement that has been afoot for decades to shelter children, not just from every possible risk of physical harm, but emotional harm as well. Mommies keep their kids out of sports activities for fear they might get hurt. They try to keep them from climbing on everything, as kids are prone to do. They don't let them play outside in the dirt, mud, and water. Playground equipment is sterilized and modified. Folks, I grew up with steel and wooden playground gear. Swings had bare chains. Slides were slick and shiny stainless steel that scorched your butt on a hot summer day. I got splinters in my hands and scraped my knees and elbows, yet somehow I survived.

Of course, I am not saying you should ignore damaged or broken equipment, but for the love of all that is Holy, your kid is not going to die from a blister, a skinned knee, or a bump to the noggin. I can't even imagine how many times I laid my bicycle over trying to jump the curb or other objects. My mom could not keep a box of Band-Aids™ in our house when I was a kid. I probably had one on my body every day from June to September. And, my grandmothers both had mecuricome and merthiolate in their medicine cabinets. Wow, did that sting!

19

Why is it okay, even preferable for your rugrats to bump, bruise and scrape themselves up? Simple, it teaches them that stupid behavior hurts and they should be more cautious in the future. It also instills in them an understanding that they are not going to die from every minor injury. They understand that pain is generally very temporary and that it is a part of living. This is not just physical toughness you are teaching them, but mental toughness as well. A bloody nose is not going to kill you; it's not even going to slow you down all that much.

In today's world we have fully grown adults who treat minor injury as a life-threatening experience. At the first sign of blood, or feeling of pain, they surrender and fold like a house of cards. They rush to the clinic for aid.

The human body is truly an amazing thing and a tough mind can direct the body through pain and discomfort. For those who have never been in a fist fight, never fallen off of a bike, never skinned their knees, the first encounter with real pain traumatizes their fragile minds and they fall apart.

Long ago the term "experience is the best teacher" was a common phrase and people understood the innate truth of it. Today, soft parents are afraid to allow their kids to have any real world experiences. They shelter them from even the slightest risk. No hiking, camping, sports, bicycles, skateboards, etc. The rationale is that when they are older the kids can decide for themselves to seek experiences and adventures. But they do not. They have been taught and conditioned that any risk is too dangerous, that they need to be sheltered and kept comfortable. And so, that has become what they seek, shelter and comfort.

Let your kids get dirty. Let them actually play with stuff with their hands. A friend of mine recently related a story about her three-year-old niece telling her that she wanted to "watch play doh". I will admit I didn't know what that was all about. My friend informed me that people put up YouTube videos of themselves making things, creations, out of Play-Doh™ and that her niece would watch the Play-Doh videos on her mommy's phone. Sweet Buddha on a Rubber Raft! Buy the kid some real Play-Doh. Sit them down at the kitchen table and let them play with it.

A similar situation that seemed all too incredible to me was the MineCraft (a digital map building game) YouTube videos. My son, Zach, told that there were videos where you could simply watch people play / build the MineCraft map worlds. There are even YouTube videos where you watch other people playing video games.

Holy Hell people! We have kids today so lazy and sluggish that they cannot even play their own video games. They have to watch other people do it for them. What kind of generation of oxygen-thieves are we raising? At least I played my own Atari Asteroids and Space Invaders games.

Beneficial Activities

Grappling activities, such as collegiate-style wrestling or jiu jitsu, are fantastic ways to introduce young people, even as young as five or six, to physical contact without the impact or striking aspect. A well-taught and structured grappling sport teaches kids not to fear contact with other humans. They learn coordination, balance, agility, and other physical skills. Their mind learns that just because someone might grab a hold of them or even knock them down, they are not going to die, nor do they simply have to surrender and give up.

Skill at grappling teaches genuine physical and mental confidence. This is a confidence that is carried off the mat and into their daily lives. Grappling sports also develop

21

problem solving skills and, as importantly as anything else, they teach kids how to deal with defeat.

In our modern soft, dare I say cowardly, world, children are sheltered from any type of defeat or loss. The insidious and poisonous trend of "no score" soccer and participation trophy sports robs young people of the experience of losing. Having never experienced a loss or a disappointment as a child, that person is devastated when they grow up and encounter a loss or failure as an adult.

Adults who were given participation trophies or played "no score" games as children, have weak minds. When faced with the cold reality of the real world, they have no coping skills on which to fall back. A loss or a disappointment becomes a mentally devastating event. They cannot fathom the "unfairness" of it all and they seek someone who will "fix it" and make everything "fair and equal". In short they become the perfect victim. Their loss is not due to the fact that they did not work hard or try their best, no it is because someone else cheated or the situation was "unfair". These sheltered kids now become bitter adults. They focus not on self-improvement, but instead wallow in self-pity and the loss eats away at them. These sheltered kids never learned to "shake it off" and try harder next time.

You say grappling sports or other team sports are not for your kids? Fine, get their little butts to the pool and teach them to swim. The water does not give a crap about their self-esteem or feelings. They will either learn to defeat the water or the water will defeat them. Have you ever watched a four or five-year-old child who is a strong swimmer? They are fearless. It matters not one bit to them that the water is three times deeper than they are tall. They jump in with reckless abandon with a genuine confidence that they can stay afloat and move about the water with skill. The fear they had of drowning on day one is long forgotten. It does not even occur to them to be scared.

When your child is mature enough the control their impulses and follow instructions (that varies with every kid) they can, and should, be introduced to the shooting sports. Archery is a fantastic way to introduce elementary age kids to the shooting sports. Archery teaches not just physical coordination and skill, but mental discipline as well. A young archer absolutely must still their body and focus on the physical technique they have been taught. The target does not give one whit about their self-esteem or the fact that mommy thinks they are special. Their arrows will either go in the center of the target because they did it right or they will not because they did not apply the lessons learned.

If the young archer genuinely desires to hit the target they must discipline their bodies to do everything right. No one can shoot the arrows for them. When the arrow hits the mark, the young person is filled with a sense of genuine accomplishment and real self-esteem, the kind you cannot pass out in the form of a participation trophy or ribbon. Before long, the kids will begin to challenge themselves. They will shoot at smaller targets or move the target farther away. You will not have to tell them; they will desire the challenge.

Older kids can mimic the aforementioned lessons while using a rifle, a handgun, or a shotgun. Again, the orange clay target flying across the sky does not take into account the shooters feelings. It can only be broken by a shooter that has disciplined themselves and applied what they were taught. A kid who breaks only three of 25 clays will want to break four the next time, then five, then six and so on.

As a seasoned firearms instructor, the most difficult part of teaching adults to shoot a rifle or pistol is not the physical motions or movement. No, the toughest part is getting the adult shooter to actually discipline their minds to apply the lessons and do what they were taught. Precision shooting is perhaps ten percent physical and ninety percent mental. The best long distance shooters in the world are those with a calm and confident mind.

A 19-year-old Army private who spent their entire youth being awarded participation trophies and being schooled about their feelings and self-esteem is a tremendously difficult person to teach to shoot. They expect success with the first shot and are frustrated to see that the target is a random mess of bullet holes. Far too often, the first response of these perfectly conditioned victims is to blame the instructor for not "teaching them right". Again, no one can fire the shot for you, you must do it yourself.

Chapter 2

Physical Readiness and Life Experience

When it comes to training up our Honey Badgers, the mind and the body work in concert. Most physical activities, in addition to training the body, help to train the mind. Dedicated followers of Student of the Gun are familiar with Jarrad, my oldest son. We taught Jarrad to swim at age four. He went from clinging to his mother's side in the pool to jumping into water far over his head in a few short months. Before long he was a fearless swimmer.

Of course, not everyone has easy access to a swimming pool. However, swimming is an excellent means of teaching young children physical coordination without ever having to explain the "why" behind it. If you cannot coordinate your body movements in the water, you cannot learn to swim. It is really very simple. Also, without a doubt, swimming is an excellent full body exercise.

We let Jarrad play outside, ride a bike, play in the rain, sled ride, etc., and more than once he came home filthy, wet, covered in mud. Somehow he survived this inhuman experience. If you are a child of the sixties, seventies, or even the eighties, you probably spent the majority of your summer vacation running around and getting dirty. At least we boys did. The girls in my neighborhood ran in their own packs. They rode pink bikes adorned with baskets and bells, but they were out there playing in the sunshine.

Grappling

When Jarrad was in the Second grade, I suppose he was seven, his mother heard about the "Attack Team" a local junior league wrestling squad. The team met two to three times a week in the high school wrestling room during the traditional collegiate wrestling season in Ohio. He took to it like a fish to water.

It was not long before Jarrad was taking first place in local and regional matches. During the few years he was with the Attack Team he qualified to the State Finals and placed in the top three several years in a row. He wrestled in middle school and then when he was in high school he discovered Shingitai Jujitsu.

John Saylor is a champion national and international judo competitor and a former coach at the U.S. Olympic Training Center in Colorado. Shingitai Jujitsu is a Japanese based martial arts, as opposed to the currently popular Brazilian form. Jarrad studied under Coach Saylor from age 16 to 18. The training program included not just grappling and submissions, but also throws and falling. Yes, it is important to know how to fall or take a throw without being injured. Saylor also taught striking and the physical conditioning.

Shooting Sports

Concurrently to his grappling and jujitsu training, Jarrad got involved in the 4H Shooting Sports program in the year 2000 when a local club formed in our county. I read a story in the area newspaper about the new 4H club and took Jarrad to a fundraiser they were having at a sportsmen's club. The die was immediately cast. I attended Adult Volunteer Training that spring and Jarrad, then Paxton, and finally Zachary became 4H members.

The highlight of our year from 2000 to 2014 was the annual Shooting Education Camp held each summer for youths ages 11 to 18. I taught at the camp and all of my kids participated in various disciplines, including Archery,

Shotgun, Muzzle loading, Living History, Pistol, and Rifle. My kids had the opportunity to be taught and coached by wonderfully talented, patient and experienced adult 4H volunteers.

While gun culture folks look first at the firearms side of the shooting sports camp, the experience was about far more than simply learning to use guns and bows. The 4H Shooting Sports program is, first and foremost, a youth development organization. It is through the mechanism of shooting firearms and archery gear that we instill self-discipline, personal maturity, sportsmanship, genuine self-confidence, and physical coordination and skills in young people.

A natural byproduct of the shooting sports program is that young people are taught to respect, not fear, firearms. You will never meet a safer and responsible shooter than a 4H trained and educated boy or girl. These boys and girls soon grow to be men and women with a healthy appreciation of what it takes, not just to be successful with a bow or rifle but, to be successful in life. I am honored to still be in touch with many of my 4H "kids" who are now productive adult members of their communities.

The 4H program is not perfect. You must closely monitor any organization that is headed up by college intellectual types. While I was working on this book I had the opportunity to talk with a mom who was a 4H Shooting Sports volunteer instructor. She explained to me that the 4H SS Coordinator insisted that all the kids be divided into six person shooting "squads". At the end of the season the coordinator set up an award ceremony where the 4H shooters were given a trophy or ribbon from 1st to 6th place. Yep, everyone who showed up got an award at the end.

In a rational world, giving out six place awards to six people would seem to be lunatic nonsense. However, to the modern collegiate hippie mind, giving an award to everyone is a form of wonderful fairness. I'm sure the kid who got a 6th place ribbon out of six kids will cherish that achievement for the rest of their life. Hell, they will probably be telling that story of triumph to their grandkids. (NOT)

Farm Work

I understand everyone's circumstances will vary. I am merely relating what worked for us. When you consider Jarrad as an adult, you can consider some of the influences that he had while growing up. Your situation will naturally be unique.

When I was a teenager we lived on a small farm in Ohio. I learned to appreciate the value of hard physical labor and the responsibility associated with caring for livestock. The cows, chickens, hogs and horses needed water and food, every day, not just when you were feeling up to it. We didn't have dairy cows, but a good friend of mine lived on a dairy farm. Many were the times that I helped him finish the evening milking chores so we could go out and see a movie, chase girls and find other ways to occupy our teenaged selves.

Summers were occupied not just with killing tin cans and ground hogs with .22 rifles, but with bailing hay and splitting wood for the wood burning stoves. One year I showed a market hog at the county fair through my local 4H group (there was no 4H Shooting Sports when I was young).

Those teenage years taught me a tremendous respect for farmers and those who work the land. Vacations for those men and women were rare. Days off only came when you were too sick to work and then chores, etc. had to be made up when you were well again. Farm communities are genuine communities in the traditional sense. Small farms often survived because neighbors helped each other. They lent tractors and equipment when yours was broken and in the shop. If a farmer broke an arm or leg, others would help with chores as best they could.

I learned physical skills on the farm that I would not have learned in the city. For instance, I learned not only how to ride a horse, but how to put the bridle and saddle on it properly. You only have to fall off once because the saddle was not cinched down to learn that lesson.

Additionally, I learned how to catch a loose hog that is running through your mother's garden tearing it up with every step. (The answer is; you chase it as fast as you can and dive with all of your might to catch a hold of that sucker's rear legs. There is no room for timidity when it comes to catching a hog.)

I learned how to drive a tractor and then a pickup truck on the back dirt roads. Yes, I was driving around the county for a good year or more before the state actually gave me a plastic card with my picture on it. (*Note: the author does not endorse the violation of traffic laws) I learned that a 1972 Oldsmobile can, indeed, be driven through the outer edge of a cornfield and survive with nary a scratch. (Not intentionally, but stuff happens) You simply need to crawl up underneath it and pull the corn stalks out the next morning.

Farm or not, it is a good idea to teach young people the proper way to use hand tools and then power tools later on. Much to my father's frustration, as soon as I figured out how to pound a nail and then pull it out if need be with a claw hammer, I was a hammering fool. I built forts and go cart type monstrosities. For Christmas one year my parents bought me an electric jigsaw. I was able to cut intricate shapes from wood and, yes, I still have all of my fingers.

When we moved to the farm the entire house was heated with wood-burning stoves. I learned to use a chainsaw to fell dead trees and cut logs into manageable sections. The scars from the chainsaw bite on my right arm have faded over the last three decades and can barely be seen. It was a minor wound and sounded much worse to my, at the time, girlfriend over the phone. "Paul can't come to the phone now, he cut his arm with the chainsaw." I did survive, thank you for your concern. I also learned to be more sure of my footing when using that tool.

The wood-burning heat system taught me to hate the steel wedge and sledge hammer combination for splitting logs. The standard wood splitting maul from the hardware store was not much better. We went through at least three maul handles the first season. My mother, bless her heart, ordered a "Monster Maul" from the Mother Earth News magazine. Wow! That thing had a steel handle and could split any log I put it to. Believe me, I learned the truth behind the old saying that a wood-burning stove warms you twice, first while you are splitting the wood and then when you are burning it.

One very unique aspect of our little farm house in Ohio was the fact that we moved into it after an Amish family had moved away to a larger piece of property. Although the construction was modern, there was no electricity or running water inside. We had an outhouse and a hand operated water pump. Oil lamps provided evening light. My mom cooked most breakfasts in a cast iron skillet.

For the first six weeks or so, we made do with the Spartan facilities until we were able to get an electrician to attend to the internal wiring, socket repair and installation of a breaker box. Baths were taken by heating water on the wood stove and I learned quickly how to ensure that the outhouse was clear of spiders before taking a seat. An old coffee that contains powdered lime (calcium hydroxide) is your friend, but you need to use it cautiously. You do not want lime on your skin or in your eyes, mouth, nose, etc.

Though I do not presently live on a farm and I do have central heat in my current home, that does not diminish the lessons from my youth. If the power were to go out tomorrow, though it might be inconvenient, my family would survive just fine and those lessons from my younger days would prove, once again, to be very valuable. It is lessons like those that toughen not just the body but the mind as well

I suppose the primary theme of this chapter could be practical life experience. Considering the experiences of myself as a young person and then those of my children, I am grateful to have parents who let me get dirty, fall off of a bicycle, and also gave me the responsibility of caring for animals and doing chores that contributed to the success and stability of the household.

Many of the lessons I learned from my youth were passed down to my children. Naturally their childhood and mine was rather different. My parents weare both Registered Nurses and had medical careers. My chosen career path varied tremendously. Regardless, Nancy and I raised our kids like my parents raised me. The kids were protected, but not sheltered. They were encouraged, but not coddled. Our children were educated to understand certain dangers, not indoctrinated to live in constant fear.

Without a doubt, you are reading this book because you are sincerely interested in providing your children with the best training, education, and information that you can offer them. Chances are also high that you are an Alpha personality. You want to take charge and do things yourself. The question you must ask yourself from time to time is, "Should I stay or should I go?" As in, should you let the wrestling coach handle practice while you go get coffee? Does the shotgun instructor have it under control without your input?

Let me offer an example. I have been a firearms and tactics instructor of one sort or another since 1990. When my wife expressed interest in getting her concealed carry permit I went out and found an instructor that I trusted and let him teach her. She came home after the first day excited. She told me "He said we should do *this*" or "He told us never to do *that*". I laughed at her and remarked "I have been saying that for years." "Well, I don't remember you ever saying that." she retorted.

There are times when you should be educating and teaching your kids and then there are times when it is best to walk away and allow someone else to do it. In my professional life I have been honored to call many world class trainers and instructors my friends. My Honey Badgers definitely benefited from my networking.

When the time comes for your little Honey Badger to get involved in an organized activity; wrestling, martial arts, shooting sports, etc. they may learn, more and enjoy the experience more, if another mature, intelligent adult instructs them. Having your dad as your coach can be a nightmare for many kids.

Let's face it, your kids will want you to be proud of them and they will be aware that you are watching and critiquing their performance. This can lead to anxiety and make the activity less enjoyable. I would never tell you to simply abandon your kids to a stranger, but you need to know when to walk away and let the coach teach them without you looking over their shoulder.

Planting Seeds

Sometimes you simply need to plant the seed and walk away allowing it to grow. You cannot force your garden to grow by watching it constantly. Plant the seed in fertile ground, give it water and sunshine, and it will grow without coercion.

Often, the seeds of wisdom you plant may take a long time to grow and produce fruit. I recall during my time in the Marine Corp, when I was around 20 or 21 years old, that a wisdom seed sprouted. A situation occurred and I remembered my dad having given me advice that applied to that exact circumstance. It was as if he had given me a screwdriver ten years prior and I was just encountering a loose screw.

I called my dad soon after and told him that his advice from years earlier had benefitted me. Always humble, my father admitted that he did not recall having offered that specific counsel. Nonetheless, he had.

Keep that in mind. Your counsel and advice might not seem like it is making a difference at the time. But, like a seed, it may be lying in fertile ground awaiting the right time to grow.

33

Paxton and Zachary visit 4H Camp with daddy.

Jarrad (Center) survived the mud.

Daddy's little honey badger.

Caring for an animal helps kids learn responsibility.

Paxton excelled at shotgun sports (4H SE Camp)

18-year-old Jarrad showing no fear in the cage. (he defeated the giant)

Have a Choke and a Smile.

Instill the spirit of the honey badger in your kids and they may grow to be fearless adults.

Chapter 3

Training the Junior Honey Badgers

For decades I have been asked, "What is a good age to introduce my kids to shooting?" or "When should I get my kids involved in martial arts?" Although the following answer seems like a cop out or a half-answer, the truth of the matter is that every little crumb cruncher is different, so it depends on the kid in question. The biggest variable is the mental and physical maturity of the child we are talking about educating.

Naturally, your rugrat needs to be housebroken, I mean potty trained, before you release them to the gymnastics or tumbling class. My answer to at what age do you teach kids firearms safety is easy. When are they mentally mature enough to understand to look both ways before crossing the street and not to play with matches? That is when you teach firearms safety.

Education Principles

In keeping with our discussion of education or training, not just for kids, but for anyone, there are certain basic principles that we should acknowledge and to which we must adhere. First of all, when we are teaching humans, we move from the known to the unknown and from the basic to the complex.

Think about it like this. In order to teach a person algebra, they must first recognize and understand numbers and letters. It does not matter how hyper-intelligent and skilled the Algebra teacher is if the classroom is filled with kids who do not know their A,B,C's and 1,2,3's. In the firearms world, it is a waste of time to send someone to Sniper School if they don't understand how a bolt-action rifle functions, much less how to load it.

Using the "Known to Unknown/Basic to Complex" method, we ensure that the student has a solid base or foundation upon which to build their new skill set. Without a solid foundation to build upon you are wasting your time. Can you teach someone to repair an engine when they don't understand what a wrench is used for?

Also, regardless of the desired skill or field of endeavor, there is a hierarchy of competency or mastery that we must consider. This was explained to me by John Farnam thirty years ago when I took my first professional firearms training course.

Unconscious Incompetence: You do not know what you do not know. This is also known as blissful ignorance. Most Americans simply assume that hitting a target with a handgun is a simple process and that if need be they could perform that task on demand. We hear statements such as, "Well, I've never had any training, but if I ever had to do it I'm sure I'd know what to do." or similar delusional verbiage. Can you imagine someone saying that about piloting an airplane? "Well, I've never flown a plane, but I've seen people do it on television, how hard could it be?"

Conscious Incompetence: A student must be at this level in order for the actual education process to commence. This step is when the student realizes that they do not possess the skill or education that they are seeking and have acknowledged that fact. A young man steps into the sparring ring for the first time and is slapped with the cold reality that he does not have the skill he thought he did. Accepting conscious incompetence requires a mature mind. You accept that you need to learn, to seek out education and training.

Conscious Competence: This is the level you reach after you have dedicated yourself to your initial training and education. This is essential Boot Camp level training. As long as you consciously apply yourself and remember what you were taught, you can complete the task or demonstrate the skill. During the conscious competence phase, you run through the steps one at a time in your head. As long as you have time to think about what you should do, you can do it.

Unconscious Competence: This is the goal of all physical skills. Whether we are talking about throwing a spiral pass with a football or hitting a steel silhouette target at a thousand yards, the goal is to be able to perform the skill on demand, immediately, without having to first stop and think about it. Essentially, when you achieve the unconscious competence level you are more likely to perform correctly than incorrectly. In the firearms training world, we say that we train and then practice, not so that we can hit the target, but so that we cannot miss the target. Pause and consider that for a moment.

Junior Honey Badgers

Keeping with our discussion about raising fearless little honey badgers, let us consider that the "junior" category would come first. The age range for the juniors would be from the time they are ready to go to school to adolescence. I know the time between eleven and thirteen is awkward and this is not necessarily a hard score. Keep in mind that the education principles we considered previously apply to all, regardless of whether the subject is six years old, eighteen, or even fifty.

Fear or Respect

Let us consider fire and water for a moment. Neither fire nor water would be considered bad or evil, but both can kill you. Too much fire or water can destroy your home and bring about ruin. Too little fire or water can also kill you through hypothermia or dehydration. Fire and water, in the correct amounts, are essential for life.

We teach our children to respect fire and respect bodies of water. They respect the power of fire and water, but they do not grow up afraid of it. Children can be taught to respect powerful things; cars, electricity, power tools, firearms, etc. For example, kids should not fear cars, but they should be wary of stepping out in front of them.

When the known or basic areas are covered, we can move on to the more complex. Children are curious creatures. The world is a huge place full of new stimuli. The reason young children constantly ask questions is because of their desire to see, touch, and experience everything around them. That is natural and the way it should be.

Adults, particularly adults with professional training under their belts, should understand the value of situational awareness. Being aware of what is going on around you can be the difference between a scary near miss and a head on collision. Drivers who keep their heads up and pay attention have close encounters, those who do not, regularly run into things, including other cars.

Awareness Game

Children are naturally curious and constantly looking around. We can use that aptitude to train them to be skilled observers and foster situational awareness. When my children were elementary school age we started playing the Awareness Game. Kids like games, game are fun, not grim or serious. If you make the exercise a grim, life and death situation, your kids will be turned off.

The Awareness Game can be called anything you like, but it works like this; wherever it is that you happen to reside, there is likely a certain fashion trend or popular sports team. In south Mississippi a clothing line called "Southern Belle" was very popular. "Southern Belle" t-shirts came in every color under the rainbow and had a consistent theme and logo. We noticed that every time we would go shopping we would see not just one or two, but numerous, Southern Belle shirts. The kids started counting these shirts to see who could find the most before we finished our shopping trip. One of the rules was "no doubles". If I spotted a red SB shirt that was mine and you could not claim it.

Naturally, you do not need to use Southern Belle shirts, anything will do. Pittsburgh Steelers or Dallas Cowboy jerseys or shirts will work. The point of the exercise is to get the kids' heads up and out of their phone and have them paying attention to the world around them. If you really want them to get hard corps, offer a treat or reward for the most points (one shirt = one point). At the end of the shopping trip the child with the most points gets to pick a treat. No, don't be a pussy and give every kid a treat for trying, that defeats the purpose. Most of the time you just compete for bragging rights.

If you play the Awareness Game often enough, eventually "Head up and Paying attention" will be their natural state as opposed to something unusual. Your kids learn situational awareness without it being a serious lesson in which you forced them to participate. Pretty sneaky, huh?

Once you have the basic concept of the Awareness Game down you can spice it up or add variety. Nonetheless, be sure that you are keeping the game part intact. The moment it stops being enjoyable your kids will tune out. That is simply the nature of children (and far too many adults).

While I was working on this chapter I discussed the topic with my wife and partner for life, Nancy. "That's like the Colorado plate game." she reminded me. I had actually forgotten all about that.

For a short time early in our marriage we lived in Colorado. We all moved to Florida after I took an Executive Protection job in Sarasota. Jarrad had just turned four years old. Between the move from Colorado, to visiting our families in Ohio and then journeying to Florida we spent a lot of time as a young family on the road. Colorado license plates are a rarity east of the Mississippi river and it was unique to spot one.

We started playing a game where Jarrad would get a dollar for spotting a Colorado license plate before anyone else. And no, I didn't just *give* the dollars to him. If I saw it first, he did not 'win'. We were playing a type of awareness game without any ulterior motive.

Zombie Attack

It is not enough to simply see what is happening. You must act upon the stimulus your eyes have gathered. Seeing the train coming in not enough, you need to step off the tracks to avoid being hit.

The next game is a play on the popularity of all the zombie apocalypse movies and TV shows; "Zombie Attack." Kids all know instinctively that you cannot allow a zombie to get near you, touch you or bite you. You need to get away from the zombies or hide from them, and you need to do it quickly.

I will admit that I modified this game from the social media game of "The Object on your Right/Left is your Zombie Apocalypse Weapon". In the Zombie Attack game your kids have to quickly decide to either run to get away or to hide, but they must make a decision.

Mom or dad are the controllers in this game. Without any warning, you say "Zombie Attack" loudly enough that all the kids can hear it. The kids then have to freeze, survey their surroundings and tell you whether or not they are going to run or hide. Then they tell you either where they are going to run to or hide, and why.

One of the runaway rules I have is that you cannot run out of the same door you came in, that's where the zombies are entering. As for hiding places, half-hiding does not count, i.e.: crawling under a standard table (where the zombie could see you if they looked down) is half-hiding.

If you have multiple children, in the zombie game the youngest always gets to go first. If not, the youngest will be self-conscious and attempt to mirror the older kids' answers. The point of the game is obviously to provide a fun/enjoyable way to teach kids rapid decision making skills and basic safety and security. This also teaches them to quickly survey their surroundings and find an exit other than the main entry/exit doors.

In a genuine emergency or crisis, such as a fire, the sheep will all stampede to the main entrance because that is their blind default. I should not have to explain to you the perils of being in the middle of a mob of panicked sheep who are all heading to the front door at the same time.

Though my children are no longer little kids, we will play a similar game. Sitting at a restaurant table I'll say "Point to the nearest exit." They know from experience that the door we came in is off limits. We also have a similar game regarding "cover", as in use of cover to stop bullets from impacting your body. Find the nearest cover.

Quite naturally, in a genuine emergency you want your kids to stay close to you and to listen to your commands. However, that strong desire does not negate the reality that your kids will not always be within arm's reach. How often do you let your kids go out with other kids' families? Your little crumb crunchers will eventually reach adolescence and stretch their little wings seeking some freedom. You will not always be there to keep them safe, they need to learn how to keep themselves safe if need be.

Rock Solid Foundation

If you are able to ingrain a solid awareness and survival mindset in your kids, they will take that with them wherever they go. The mindset is the foundation. Soon it will be time to teach your Honey Badgers how to bite and claw, but before they do that, they need to have a strong and fertile mind. Unlike the "helicopter" parents of today who are constantly hovering over their kids trying to shield them from the world, your Junior Honey Badgers will be ready to take on the world and the challenges it throws at them.

By this time, you should have picked up on the fact that Junior Honey Badgers are better off surviving with their wits that their fists. I don't care how much you pay the local Karate instructor and how many colored cloth belts they award to your child; a 60 pound third grader is no match for a fully grown human monster. That is not to say that I suggest that kids should just take it, far from it, but size and strength are always factors that must be considered.

Only after you are sufficiently certain that your Jr. HB is mentally mature for their age, should you introduce them to the ferocious physical techniques that allow the smaller and weaker opponent to conquer opposing foes. Teaching an eye gouge or throat smash technique to an immature young person is just begging for trouble. We do not gouge the eyes of someone who cuts in front of the lunch line or makes fun of our choice of tennis shoes. Modern cardio-Karate and strip mall Tae Kwon Do are fun exercise. But the aforementioned have almost nothing to do with the reality of mortal combat.

Reflexes, Agility, and Dexterity

Although the terms reflexes, agility, and dexterity are not identical or interchangeable, they are certainly similar enough to be discussed in the same section.

We fall back on that question, "When is a good time for my kids to start in the Martial Arts?" The realistic answer is that you, as a responsible parent, need to take realistic stock in your child's mental maturity level. Can you leave sharp knives unlocked or matches on the counter with the assurance that your kids will not play with them? Have you gauged their maturity level by giving them tasks and responsibilities? Though it may seem a bit oversimplified, if your child can care for a pet without being constantly reminded or nagged, they are exhibiting maturity. An older child that shows a healthy level of concern for the protection of younger siblings also is displaying mental maturity. They are learning to care about something besides their own comfort. Do I need to tell you how rare that is in today's world?

In the following chapter for the Senior Honey Badger, we will get into actual physical techniques and the use of tools for defense. I will leave it up to you, the parent, to decide when the material can be introduced to the younger ones, or even the older ones for that matter.

Chapter 4

Senior Honey Badger

When your little Honey Badger matures from being a cub to a young boar or sow (yes, a male HB is a boar and a female is a sow), it is time to entrust them with more knowledge and responsibility. We will assume that you have already instilled the situational awareness skills and educational principles that were previously discussed in Chapter 3. In the event that you skipped ahead to this part of the book, go back to the previous chapter and read the "Educational Principles" section. Understanding these principles is key when teaching new physical techniques to any student.

Puberty, adolescence, and the transition from teen years to adulthood can be, and are, a stressful time for our Honey Badgers. Throw in the threat of bullying, sexual assault and kidnapping, mass murders, and it is enough to make you want to lock your kids in a tower until their 18th birthday. Hiding them is not the answer. Teaching, guiding, and training them is a much better solution.

We cannot possibly sterilize the world and at some point in time our Honey Badger will be out on their own, without us to guide and protect them. This is a balancing act to be sure. Give them too much free play and they may become unruly and reckless. However, if you attempt to shelter them from every possible hazard they may feel smothered and they will begin to resent you and push away.

If you are a young parent or were raised by hippies, you may be behind the curve when it comes to training up your Honey Badger. Fear not, as long as we are all breathing and above room temperature, there is still time.

Some would tell you that teaching your children to fight only breeds the desire to fight in them. To that I say; "horse shit". A child's desire to fight, to be aggressive, or not to be so, is based upon their mentality, their mindset, not the physical skills they may or may not have. School yard bullies did not become that way because they were taught boxing or karate.

To be quite frank, your kids are less likely to become a physical or emotional bully if they do engage in fight training of some sort. Consider this, in order to excel at any type of martial endeavor, you must discipline your body to perform as you are taught. You cannot throw proper kicks or punches until your mind forces your body to do it correctly, to follow instructions.

A young Honey Badger who strives to throw the perfect right cross, round kick, judo throw, or leg lock must first master their mind and body. No coach or instructor can *force* you to execute a technique properly. Mastering a physical technique forces the HB to exercise self-control and self-discipline. Those with reckless and undisciplined minds will rarely ever go far in any martial art or other endeavor. The mind must direct the body to throw the perfect punch. Ergo, the desire to throw the perfect kick or punch teaches the young HB self-control and self-discipline.

When the time comes to choose a martial discipline, or to at least expose your HB to it, you have a serious decision to make. Martial sports, particularly westernized forms of Karate, Kung Fu, Tae Kwon Do, etc. focus on points and forms. There is nothing wrong with that, but you must be honest and understand that "Cardio Kickboxing" is a fun sport that is used as exercise, it is not designed for mortal combat.

I know, the thought of your child engaged in mortal combat makes you want to vomit. It scares the hell out of you even thinking about it. But here we are back at that crossroad; do I want to shelter my child from the evils of the world or do I want to prepare my child for them?

If your twelve-year-old daughter, or son even, is being forced into a vehicle by a 250-pound rapist, are your *feelings* going to be enough to help them survive? Will your child be able to reason with, and explain to, the two or three thugs set to beat them mercilessly, that they have been taught to "use your words"?

Regardless of all the sophistication in our lives and the shiny gadgets used to distract us, we still live in a rock and stone world. Humans bleed and die today just as they did a thousand years ago. A kick to the head while lying on the ground is just as dangerous to man in the 21st Century as it was in Biblical times. An iPhone will not lessen your pain.

All-In Fighting

William E. Fairbairn, along with his book *All-In Fighting,* was very familiar to most martial minded young men when I was growing up. *Soldier of Fortune* and all the other copycat magazines in the sixties, seventies, and eighties, frequently had articles that amounted to excerpts from the teachings and writing of Fairbairn, his onetime partner Eric Sykes, and his protégé Rex Applegate. Those three names were revered by American men.

The aforementioned warriors taught Special Operations personnel (commandos) during WWII. The men of my generation grew up reading about and, in some cases, actually learning to perform the techniques passed down by these martial mentors. When I was a young Marine I was taught bayonet fighting and sentry takedown techniques. There were no belts or sashes. We didn't have testing to advance to the next rank, we simply understood that evil men had to be dealt with in a most devastating fashion.

Flash forward to the 21st Century, so-called men in their teens and twenties are reading GQ and Maxim, if they actually read a magazine at all. Those who are of age to be the defenders of the nation are so distracted by selfish pursuits that they can barely even fathom what a Fairnbairn/Skyes Commando knife would be used for, much less how to actually use one. When I was twenty, I could not wait to get my first genuine USMC fighting knife, it was a prized possession. Today's men are obsessed with the new Galaxy Note-whatever or iPhone.

I related all of the previous information to you because this is the part of the book where I am going to introduce you to the hard reality of what Fairbairn called *All-In Fighting.* Rex Applegate called it "Kill or Get Killed" fighting and wrote a book with that very name. They understood the cold reality of mortal combat.

That kind of fighting is not for sport or points. What follows are physical techniques that, when done correctly, can allow a 100-pound woman to destroy a 200-pound man. These methods will allow your teenage son to survive a deadly encounter that would otherwise land him in the hospital or the morgue. We are not playing games here; this is deadly serious and a topic that must be addressed.

You might be thinking; "My kids take Tae Kwon Do at the local rec center, so they are good to go." Sport fighting and traditional martial art sports rely heavily on repetition of

54

technique and strength. The world is what it is, and a large, vicious attacker is unlikely to be swayed by your 12-year old's purple belt from the strip mall Karate class. I am not discounting the health and discipline benefits of sport martial arts, but we are discussing the cold reality of a vicious and horrifying attacks. Point sparring is not going to get the job done.

We must train our Honey Badgers to be ferocious when the time calls for it. We must help them to put those tools in their toolbox so the skills will be there when needed. Remember the Honey Badger is not the biggest or strongest animal, but it is the most fearless. Have you ever tried to pick up an angry cat? You outweigh the cat 20 times but the moment the cat starts hissing, clawing and biting, you let it go.

Verbalize: Make Noise!

Hand to hand defensive tactics are accompanied by loud shouting; "Stop!" We yell "stop", not "rape" or "help". Sadly, in the modern world, people have been programmed to not get involved, to avoid conflict, even if that means walking away as an innocent person is maimed or raped.

Yelling STOP accomplishes many positive tasks.

#1   Tells your attacker you are serious and not going to just take it. There is a slim chance the attacker will hesitate or call off their attack.

#2   Trains witnesses; in the aftermath the bystanders will all swear that the good guy told the bad guy to stop. That puts your HB on the moral high ground. Yes, that matters.

#3   It prevents you from holding your breath in panic mode. You cannot hold your breath and yell at the same time. Muscles need oxygen and lots of it in a fight.

#4   STOP! establishes your commitment to the fight, it is your mental "Go Code", you are giving yourself permission to act and keep driving forward.

#5   Be ferocious. Ferocious people make noise.

Strikes with Hands

*Teaching Note: Size and Strength always matter. A smaller, weaker, older person is ALWAYS better off using a tool or weapon. However, the world is an imperfect place and your only weapon might be your mind and body when you are attacked.

Open Hand techniques are used deliberately. Hard, knock-out punches with a closed fist will damage your hand in addition to injuring your opponent. You might need functioning hands to continue the fight. Professional fighters wrap their hands and protect their fists for that reason.

All strikes should be used in combination with another.

Eric Sykes is said to have finished every hand to hand combat technique by saying "...and kick them in the testicles."

1- Palm Strike

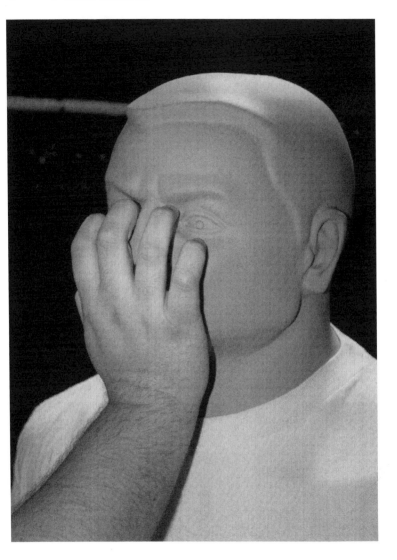

Targets: Chin and Nose

Keeping your hands open, pull your hands up to the center of your chest right under your chin. This action mirrors the startle response. To strike, drive the open palm straight out (in a straight line) from the chest to the attacker's chin. Like a well thrown jab, a straight-line, direct strike is difficult for the defender to gauge and counter. The blow to the chin should stun the mandibular nerve. (the knock-out nerve)

The Nose is the secondary target. If your blow misses the chin, because the attacker tucked at the last second, a palm strike to the nose should break it, causing pain and temporary disruption of vision. A nose strike that is done forcefully enough can fracture the bone and force it back into the cranial vault (skull) causing death, but that blow must be near perfect to do so.

Practice: Use own hand as practice target, use a partner's hand as practice target, use a heavy bag (punching bag) or a specially made training dummy.

2-   Ear Slap   Single or Double

Targets: Ears

In addition to our hearing, our ears (inner ears) control balance and equilibrium. A hard slap to one or both ears can break the eardrums and upset the attacker's balance.

An ear slap is quite elementary. Simply close the fingers to create a cup with the palm and slap the ear directly. A single slap will work if one hand is trapped or occupied but a double slap is the most effective. *This is not a knockout blow, but when done properly the attacker will be stunned or slowed to the point where follow up strikes can be landed more readily.

Practice: Use own hand as practice target, use a partner's hand as practice target, use a heavy bag (punching bag) or a specially made training dummy.

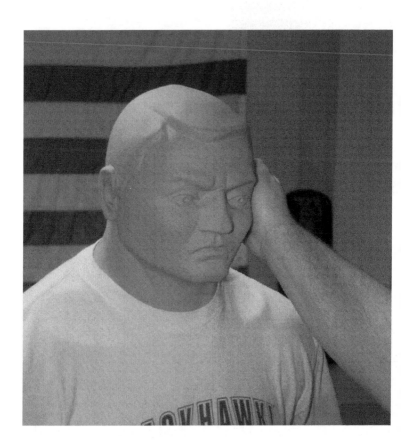

3- Eye Gouge   Single or Double

Targets: Eye Sockets

Your eyes are important, that is why God set them back in your skull and put hard bone around them. Human beings get somewhere around 80 to 85 percent of all sensory input from their eyes. The two primal fears that all humans possess are blindness (loss of sight) and suffocation.

To attack the eyes, make a hook with the thumb and, again, drive it straight forward into the eye socket. Yes, this can cause permanent damage and possible death. The only reason you should be doing this is because you are in a fight for your life. You cannot lose. You must go *All-In* and win by any means possible.

When the eye gouge technique is applied, it must be done so with commitment. Keep pushing until the attacker ceases their assault and surrenders.

Practice: Partner up with another person and practice by pressing your thumbs on their forehead, above their eyebrows. Use a specially designed training dummy with anatomically correct head.

4-   Neck Strike

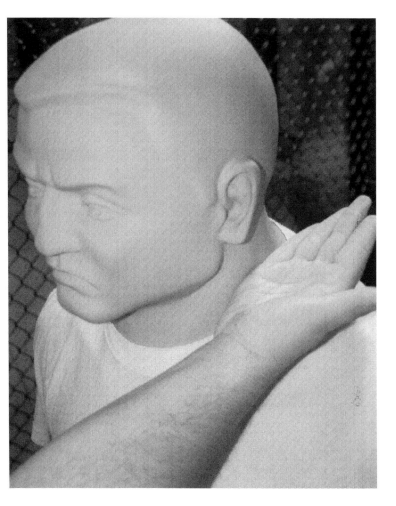

Target: Front / Side of throat

For the neck strike we will again use an open hand.
Fairbairn and Applegate suggest that the striking hand
should have the thumb straight out (90 degrees). The
meaty edge of the hand, between the base of the pinky

finger and the wrist joint, is the part that makes contact with the target.

*(*Traditional Martial Arts have you lay the thumb against the forefinger and create a bit of a cup with the palm. The Fairbairn/Applegate method seems more instinctive for the untrained.)*

Strike across with a chopping motion to the front of the attacker's throat (windpipe). Blows to the side of the neck can affect the nerves to the point where the attacker is momentarily stunned.

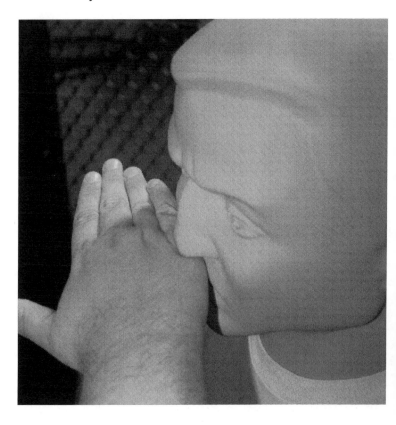

A chop from the inside (in front of the body) is not as powerful because you cannot wind up, but you do not need a lot of power to damage a windpipe. A strike from the outside is easier for the attacker to counter because they have time to prepare, but it is more powerful. Why not try both?

Should the attacker realize the strike is coming and duck their chin, a chop strike to the nose can be a very effective blow. The same goes for a strike to the side of the neck. If the attacker ducks and the blow lands on their ear, it can still be effective.

Practice: Use own hand as practice target, use a partner's hand as practice target, use a heavy bag (punching bag), focus mitts or pads, or a specially made training dummy.

Strikes with Legs

Your leg muscles are naturally larger and stronger than your arms. While you may not be as coordinated with your legs as you are with your hands and arms, with a bit of practice and training every physically able person can learn to land very effective strikes with their legs.

If your attacker cannot stand, it is extremely difficult for them to continue their attack. Take out their legs and you can escape, survive and be victorious.

Leg strikes are where having coordination, balance, and agility come into play. The balance that you learned through all of that time spent learning the martial arts or the coordination and agility gained by participating in sports pays off when it is time to use your legs to attack.

1- Foot Stomp

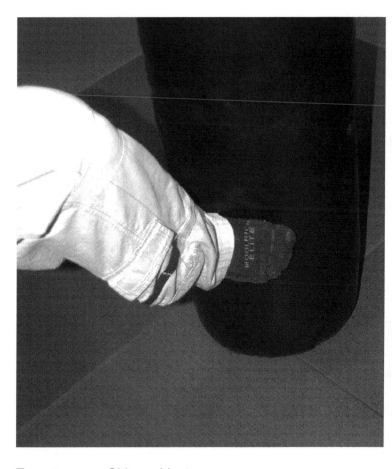

Target: Shin and Instep

Even if the attacker grabs your hands/wrists, you can still use your legs and feet. The foot stomp, or stomp kick, is an extremely effective and useful weapon in your arsenal. A person need not be particularly large or strong to effectively use a stomp kick.

To execute the foot stomp technique, lift your foot (your choice, practice with both) up approximately 12 inches off the ground. Angle your toes outward and stomp down ferociously on to the attacker's shin. The force and momentum should carry your foot down onto their instep as a secondary target. Repeat the process until achieving the desired effect and follow with another strike.

Practice: Use the doorframe of any open doorway, use a floor-length heavy bag (Muay Thai bag) or football tackling dummy held by a training partner.

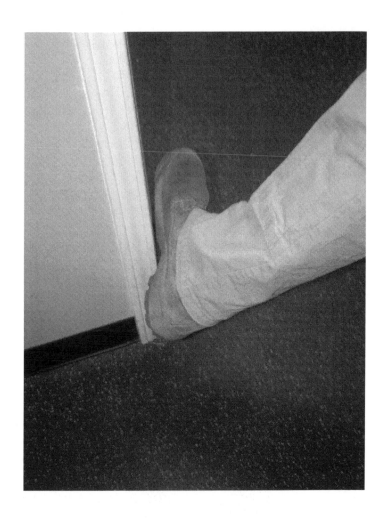

Door frame practice

2-   Knee Thrust

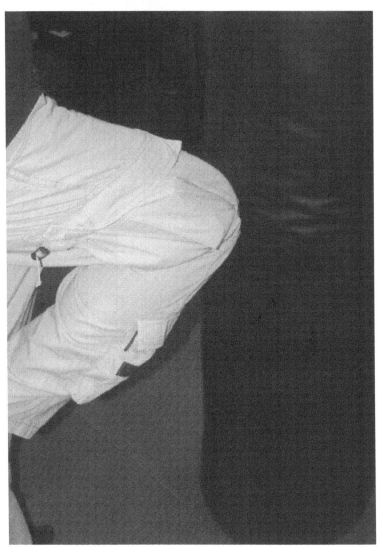

Target: Groin (primary) Inner and Outer legs (secondary)

This technique is as old as time itself. A knee to the groin is not exactly a secret ninja tactic. As such, an experienced bad guy will likely be on the lookout for a groin attack. Men like to protect their balls. This is simply a fact of life.

A knee thrust into the groin is a preferred follow up from a hand strike technique or the stomp kick. Essentially, you distract the attacker with something and then go for the nuts. That is not to say that a groin attack cannot be your first attack, just understand that most men will be on the lookout, even subconsciously, for a knee to the nuts.

Practice: Use a heavy bag, an impact shield held by a training partner, slow deliberate practice with partner wearing groin protection.

Less-than-Lethal Strikes

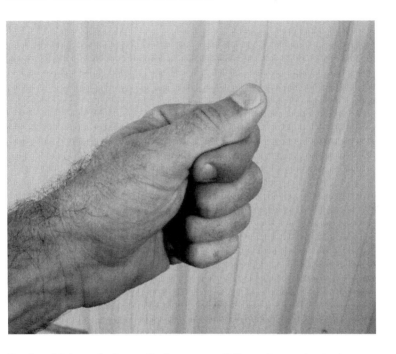

It should be obvious that some of the above techniques, when modified slightly, can be used for a less-than-lethal application. A single-handed ear slap or a chop strike to the outer neck or clavicle area are not likely to cause death or permanent harm but can be very effective as attitude adjusters. Little girls have been adjusting little boys' attitudes with a knee to the groin for as long as there have been little boys.

One attitude adjuster that I taught Jarrad when he was junior high school age was the "thumb poke". Make a fist and rather than curl the thumb over as you would with a punch, lay the thumb into the fold of the index finger. This supports the thumb and allows you to jab or poke with the tip of the thumb without injuring yourself.

The primary target for the thumb poke is the ribs. Practice on each other. It hurts. This is pain compliance and not to be used in a life and death struggle. The thumb poke is reserved for those times when you need to do something physical, but the hardcore strikes would be too much.

*There are certainly many more methods and techniques that could be taught to your HB. The physical techniques presented herein were done so because they are simple, straight forward, and easy to teach and put to use. Martial gurus in the audience are cautioned not to take the simple and make it complex. Yes, we do that.

Chapter 5

Claws and Fangs: Adding Tools

As mentioned previously, size and strength are always factors to be considered. In a fight it is preferable to arm yourself with some type of tool/weapon. When discussing our little Honey Badgers, training with and using a firearm for self-defense is another book all to itself. Even if your 15-year-old son or daughter is a competent and experienced shooter, they cannot legally carry a firearm outside of your home.

Unfortunately, when our children leave our protection they often enter areas where they are disarmed by regulation. Even low end use of force tools are viewed as "weapons" and prohibited. As the HB ages and matures their tools should mature with them.

What follows is a consideration of less-than-lethal or alternative use of force tools that the HB can be taught to use. The first two; pepper spray and the Taser will more than likely be prohibited on school grounds. Fear not, there is more than one way to skin a cat.

Author's Note: For the love of all that is Holy, stop buying handheld stun guns and giving them to your daughters "...for, just in case." Handheld stun guns are crap.

Pepper Spray

For over two decades I've been teaching police officers and citizens to properly use Oleoresin Capsicum (pepper spray) as an alternate use of force tool. When it comes down to dollars versus effectiveness, a genuine OC product is a bargain at twice the price.

Pepper spray is a LOW end use of less-than-lethal force. Permanent injury or scarring is essentially a non-issue.

Yes, it hurts and it hurts a lot, but after liberal amounts of cold water and open air, the receiver of the OC will be back to normal. They should have no bruises, broken bones or scars. Pepper spray also allows you to keep your distance from an attacker and works without requiring physical contact.

The best products to purchase are those carried by police agencies. These products, such as the ones from FOX or Guardian are higher quality than the cheap products sold at flea markets or the local gas station. Do not bet your safety on a $9 piece of crap on a spindle rack at a truck stop. Spend the money and buy a quality product; $20 is a good range.

While we are on the subject of purchasing pepper spray, it is inexpensive enough that you can by two identical units, one to carry and one to test (practice with). If the OC product is new to you, it is always a good idea to take it outside and try it out. You need to have some idea of the size of the spray pattern and how far it will travel. It you are underwhelmed by the product, do not carry it. Buy something else.

Pepper spray is not instantaneous (count three 'Mississippi') and is affected by high wind. OC is a Less-than-Lethal tool. If an attacker is using a knife, baseball bat, or firearm, pepper spray is not the preferred choice. But, for the bully, the annoying drunk, or panhandler who refuses to take no for an answer, it just might be the best medicine.

Modern Tasers

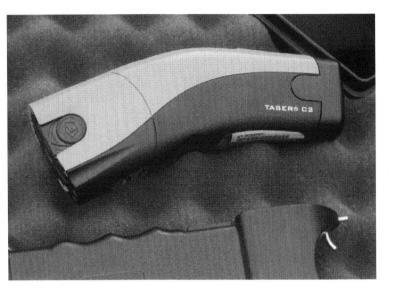

The modern Taser should not be confused with a handheld "stun gun". Products from Taser, Inc. are high-tech subject control devices and they are tremendously effective less-than-lethal tools. In most jurisdictions Tasers are perfectly legal for citizens to own and use but you should check your state's laws.

The downside to the Taser unit is expense and their single shot capability. As a high tech tool they tend to be rather pricey. While the cartridges are easy to replace, doing so in the middle of an attack is not at all practical. If one or both of the wire-tethered probes misses the mark you'll need to move on to something else, such as the contact stun.

The upside of the Taser is the fact that it is, like pepper spray, a distance weapon. Compare that to the marginally effective handheld units that require physical contact. The Taser works and works very well. Even the biggest, meanest, craziest attacker will succumb to the high voltage when used properly.

Fighting Flashlights

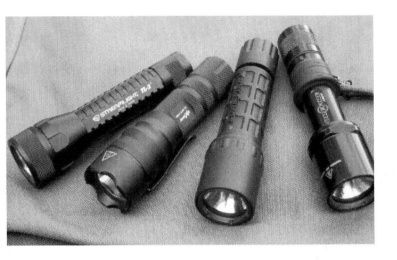

The current models of handheld flashlights, or tactical lights if you will, are at the pinnacle of modern technology. White LED lights housed in aluminum or high-strength polymer bodies with a tailcap, push-button switch can be excellent alternative use of force tools.

Because the light has some other purpose besides being a weapon it is permissible in otherwise "Weapon Free Zones". Handheld lights are allowed on airplanes whereas an aluminum mini-baton is not. Also, because it's an illuminating tool, not just a stick with which to hit people, you will actually carry it all the time.

As a force option, the light has two primary uses. First, shining a bright light at a potential threat along with the verbal command "STOP!" lets them know you mean business and are not an easy mark. If the aggressor ignores the light and keeps coming you know immediately they are a genuine threat and the rigid body of the light can be used as a striking tool.

Every prepared person should have some type of compact, but powerful, flashlight on their person at all times. You never know when you will find yourself in the dark. Think of it as a rescue tool that can be used to rescue yourself and others.

Tactical Pens

Although many self-defense gurus will dismiss the "tactical pen" as a gimmick, they fall into the category of being something other than a metal stick to hit people. Modern aluminum and Titanium pens are high-quality writing instruments. Many are decorative and blend with your daily dress. Again, like the flashlight, a pen can be carried in otherwise non-permissive environments and because it has another purpose other than hitting people, it's an object you'll want to carry.

Although they require more training and skill to use as a defensive tool than pepper spray or a Taser, few businesses will ban their employees from carrying a pen. In the hands of a person with moderate training and skill, the tactical pen can be used as an effective less-than-lethal defensive tool.

For Honey Badgers that must protect themselves in school, what better tool to have than a high quality "tactical pen"? Certainly, even the most liberal bleeding heart member of the local teacher's union could not object to your daughter having a pink anodize aluminum pen on her person.

Targets

OC-   The target for OC/pepper spray in the face. Cover the attacker's eyes, nose, and mouth with it. Simple enough, right?

Taser-   With a Taser you aim at center mass of the person attacking you. The barbed, wire-tethered probes will spread out and stick in the bad guy. (Taser, Inc. has a great deal of training material)

Lights/Pens- The targets for the lights and pens are essentially the same as for the empty handed strikes we discussed early on in the book; eyes, nose, throat, side of neck / clavicle. For less-than-lethal "leave me alone" strikes, the pen or light can be jabbed into the ribs like the aforementioned thumb. Also, any hand that grabs our Honey Badger can, and should be, smashed firmly with the light or pen.

Regardless of the tool or tools with which you choose to equip your own Honey Badger, it is essential that you teach them, work with them, prepare them for the use of the chosen tools. One of the most negligent behaviors of modern men is the purchasing and gifting of gadgets, particularly for the women in their lives.

How often have you heard of a father buying a handheld stun gun and giving it to his college bound daughter? "Here you go honey, I bought you this, just in case." You would be better off giving them a solid rock, at least they could do some damage with that. The college bound daughter will almost immediately toss the stun gun in the bottom of their backpack or stick it in a drawer never to be thought of again.

The same applies to pepper spray, etc. Handing someone an object and simply expecting them to have confidence in it during the crisis of an attack is ridiculous. Most often they will forget they even have it until the fight is over. Keyring pepper spray is a stupid idea. It immediately becomes a key fob and is forgotten as a defensive tool. Most keyring units are too small to be effective.

Chapter 6

The Balance

"Having a dad is like having a ticket to manhood. Without a dad, it is like walking around with a blindfold trying to find your way." -M, a Student of the Gun

Smother or Abandon

We have discussed "helicopter parents", those who constantly hover over their kids, refusing to allow them to get dirty or stretch their legs and experience some independence. This type of parenting is naturally counter-productive if we hope to have strong, independent children one day.

However, we do not wish to push our little badgers out of the hole and tell them to just deal with whatever happens to come their way. The premise of this book is to help you to prepare your little Honey Badgers for the big ugly world out there, to guide them, to teach them to protect themselves.

What I wish to discuss in this closing chapter is the balance that we must all seek between smothering our kids and tossing them out of the nest to fend for themselves like Spartan boys. Children need, nay they crave, structure and guidance. Far too many modern adults feel that it is their responsibility to be their kid's friend. I'm not saying you should not have a friendly relationship with your kids, but your kids need you to be a parent first.

I was listening to a radio show recently and heard a single mother talking about how she gave her ten-year-old son freedom to make his own choices and that they had conversations about choices. It is that kind of "touchy, feely" nonsense that has led us to the point we are in as a nation.

Our country is populated by young adults who were raised to simply make their own choices, void of structure, discipline, and the requirement to deal with the consequences of their actions. These kids think that their feelings trump their actions, or inactions, and that somehow someone will make it all better for them if they screw up.

My children were not perfect and neither were we as parents. The kids tested us, made bad choices on occasion and were disciplined for those bad choices. Now that our youngest child is 18 years old, we have the opportunity to examine how they interact with others as adults and how they behave on their own in the real world.

Regarding our children, both Ms. Nancy and I can say with honesty that, despite the fact that our kids do frustrate us sometimes, they are indeed good people. There are few compliments more gratifying than for other adults to tell you how mature your kids are and how much they enjoy their company. We have received those compliments numerous times and smiled with pride.

The balance you must discover is that balance between being overprotective and leaving your kids to sink or swim. Children must learn to deal with problems on their own, this much is true. If you fix every little issue your child encounters, they will never learn to fend for themselves. Nonetheless, there are problems and troubles that no child should have to deal with on their own.

School bullying is one of those issues. In our modern school system, we have both juvenile bullying by peers and we have the psychological terrorism inflicted on our children by the school staff. A one on one confrontation between 12 year olds is something your Honey Badger can be taught to manage. However, group bullying or intimidation by teachers, principals, and staff are problems that no child should be left to deal with alone.

As children move into puberty and adolescence, their bodies are flooded with testosterone, estrogen; basically their hormones begin racing. Kids become moodier and emotional and that is totally natural. The dangerous part of the situation is that we as parents may chalk up their depression, anxiety, and mood swings as "growing pains". There may be something else going on in their life that is causing them mental anguish.

A middle school girl who is being bullied may come home and take out her frustration on her siblings or parents. She might become withdrawn and seek to spend all day in her room with the door closed. Mom and dad may believe this is just "a phase" and that she will grow out of it.

Young children tell you everything that comes to their minds. Then, when they hit puberty, they stop telling you anything. This is the time that you need to be a parent, a guardian and a protector. You must deliberately engage your Honey Badger. No, it is not at all easy to talk to pubescent girls or boys, but it must be done. Kids will hold it in and try to solve their own problems, even problems that they do not have the capacity to fix. This is where you as the parent must make the judgment to let them fix the problem or help them realize that this issue is too great for them handle.

If you choose to send your children to public school, yes it is a choice in the United States of America, you must be vigilant. Please understand that you do not have to send your kids to the Socialist Indoctrination Centers we laughingly call schools. But, if you do make the aforementioned choice, you have to prepare your kids to deal with both peer bullying and staff intimidation.

When Jarrad was finishing his Senior year in High School, we gave him a wallet sized card to keep with him at all times. The short, but to the point, card stated that the administration and staff were advised that they were under no circumstances allowed to seize or withhold personal property, search Jarrad's person or property without law enforcement being present, nor were they to detain or question Jarrad without notification of the parents (us).

You may think this tact a bit extreme. Need I remind you of the numerous cases today where children were taken to an office and held for questioning in excess of an hour or more before parents were notified? Middle school girls have been humiliated by strip searches in our public schools. Children have been removed from the school grounds and taken to another facility before parents were notified. During more than one incident a child was held so long in isolation that they urinated on themselves and/or broke down in tears.

The wallet card proved a valid precaution when a teacher tried to intimidate Jarrad and step beyond her authority. One day Jarrad was standing at his locker between classes. He took his mobile phone out to look at it. A teacher walked up behind him, snatched the phone out of his hand and said, "No phones in school. I'm keeping this." The actual rule was not about possession of a mobile phone on school grounds. The rule stated that students were prohibited from taking their phones to and from classes.

Jarrad pulled the card out of his wallet and said "You had better read this first." The teacher in question begrudgingly handed Jarrad's phone back to him and muttered some face-saving threat that she had better never see the phone again or else.

You, as the mature adult parent, need to constantly weigh your actions to ensure you are neither smothering your Honey Badger nor abandoning them to fight the wolves alone. Yes, it takes effort and commitment, but aren't your kids worth it?

Take Interest

I know that it is hard to fathom some of the pop culture nonsense that your kids seem to embrace. Every generation deals with that. My grandparents did not like the Beatles. My parents did not like Kiss. I do not understand the draw of M&M (the rappist, not the candy).

When I was about 13 years old I discovered Dungeons & Dragons. A local hobby store sold the game, dice, and hundreds of little lead figures that you could paint. I would spend hours in that hobby store deciding which warrior, dwarf, or elf I would buy next with the couple of dollars in my pocket.

My parents did not "get" D&D and most of the Church leaders at the time thought it was witchcraft or devil worship. Of course, D&D is mild child's play compared to what our kids are exposed to today. D&D for me was simply living out the Hobbit or Lord of the Rings in a game format.

91

Even though my folks really did not care for, or understand, my fascination, they indulged my Dungeons & Dragons obsession. I can recall my dad sitting down at the dining room table with my siblings and me and letting me lead him through a game of D&D. It was so new to me that I hardly knew what I was doing, but he patiently endured. I gained a lot of respect and admiration for my dad from that experience. It must have been a mild form of torture for him to sit and listen to me go through all the intricacies but he did it because he loved me.

Life Balance

Balance applies to your whole life. Japan's most famous swordsman, Miyamoto Musashi, advised that a true warrior must be skilled in the healing arts as well as the killing arts. Your Honey Badgers should be encouraged to study music, poetry and classical writing, art, etc. the healing side of life, if you will.

I believe we can agree that the samurai were some of the most fearless warriors in the world. The samurai studied calligraphy, the art of the tea ceremony, painting, etc. Their lives contained balance. One of the greatest problems with young people today is that they have no balance. Their lives are consumed by selfish, hedonistic pursuits. Self-protection, security, and the preservation of their community and country are all concepts foreign to most of the youth in our nation today.

Many short-sighted people may encounter this book and believe it is all about turning kids into vicious little fighters. Fighting is only a part of the equation. The Honey Badger is the most feared animal not because it always attacks, but because it has the confidence to attack if need be. You see, Honey Badger has a genuine confidence, not some hippie form of self-esteem. Honey Badger knows how to handle him or herself and that confidence is projected out to the entire world.

What today's young people are missing is the balance of self-discipline and a sense of genuine confidence. They do not have the self-confidence that comes from the knowledge that they can be fearless and ferocious if the situation calls for it, as well as being merciful and kind.
-
When modern hipster parents shelter their kids from any potential physical or mental discomfort, they eliminate any type of balance. Children who are bright, intelligent, can master a musical instrument or a foreign language, but without a genuine confidence that they can solve problems and protect themselves from aggression, will be without balance in their lives.

Intelligent, educated, and creative young adults who have no sense of genuine self-confidence will always feel that it is someone else's job to ensure that they feel safe and secure. These people become progressive liberals. They cry out for the government to solve every problem or issue they encounter. Even if they are personally safe, they feel that it is the role of government to make everyone's life fair and equal.

This is why seemingly intelligent and educated adults favor gun control laws, environmental laws, hate-speech laws, etc. Deep inside, under their pseudo-intellectual facade, these liberal hippies have a genuine insecurity. They do not understand what it takes to ensure their own safety and solve their own problems. The entire concept of self-determination and problem solving is foreign to them. Their mommies and daddies sheltered them and prevented them from having balance in their lives. Now the liberals look to a new mommy, the government, to solve the world's problems.

When it comes to preserving the United States of America as a Representative Republic, my parents' generation, the Baby Boomers, are the ones who brought us to this impasse with their selfish, spoiled brat attitudes. The people of my generation, those who were born and raised during the Cold War, have been far too reasonable and tolerant of weakness and government overreach. If the nation is going to be preserved, it must be saved by my children and theirs.

Only by instilling the spirit of the Honey Badger into our children can we hope to equip them mentally for the grave challenges that lie ahead of them. We will not always be there to fight their battles for them and we may be gone when the greatest battle arrives.

I am truly humbled by your investment in this text. I pray that this book will give you much to think about, that it will encourage you, and bring you comfort. Most importantly, I hope that you are now on the right path to give your little Honey Badger genuine balance in their life.

Epilogue

While I was working on the final edit for this manuscript I finished reading a book written by my friend Fredrick "Cork" Graham, *The Bamboo Chest: An Adventure in Healing the Trauma of War.* As I finished the last page I realized that there were lessons in his book that I needed to relate here.

Without getting into too much detail about the story, at age 18, Cork decided that he wanted to be a Combat Photojournalist. He bought a plane ticket to Thailand with the intension of covering the still ongoing border struggles and skirmishes in and around Vietnam, Cambodia and Laos. It was 1983 at the time.

Chasing after what seemed to be a newsworthy story, Cork found himself on an island held by the Socialist Republic of Vietnam. In short order, the young man was captured by the Communist Party militia and subsequently imprisoned for nearly a year before his family was forced to pay a ransom to the SRV to secure his release.

Cork celebrated his 19th birthday in a communist political prison. Graham was beaten often as an arbitrary punishment. He was interrogated continuously to attempt to force a confession for being a spy. Cork was subjected to sleep-depravation and he was forced to eat food containing maggots and live ants or starve. (Eventually his captors were motivated to roast the ants before they served them.) He was held in isolation and deprived of even sunlight for a most of his time as a prisoner.

When Cork was finally released into the welcoming arms of friendly personnel from the United States Department of State, they remarked to him how he was in much better physical and mental shape than they had anticipated.

Graham explained in his book how, during his incarceration, he had drawn upon his life experiences, training, and education to help him get through it all unbroken.

Fortunately, Cork had received a thorough education in school. He learned to speak a foreign language (French) and he studied martial arts as well as having spent time in the US Navy's ROTC program.

The martial arts training had taught him the art of meditation and Cork used it to calm his mind and find some form of tranquility from the bowels of a concrete and steel prison. Both his marital arts experience and the ROTC training helped him understand the importance of keeping his body fit regardless of the hardship.

As I put these words to paper, I thought about my youngest, Zachary, who was the same age as Cork when he was captured. I cannot imagine the anguish of having your teenage child thrown into the Hell-hole of a communist prison.

There is no way we can predict what the future holds for our children. The lessons we teach them might not seem all that critical at the time, but may be priceless to them some day.

About the Author

Paul G. Markel has worn many hats during his lifetime. He has been a U.S. Marine, Police Officer, Professional Bodyguard, and Small Arms and Tactics Instructor. Mr. Markel has been writing professionally for law enforcement and firearms periodicals for twenty plus years with hundreds upon hundreds of articles and several books in print.

Paul is the host and producer of Student of the Gun TV and Radio. Mr. Markel is also the founder of Student of the Gun University, an entity dedicated to education and enlightenment.

For more information, please visit
www.studentofthegun.com

"Professor Paul" has been teaching safe and effective firearms handling to students young and old for decades and has worked actively with the 4H Shooting Sports program. Paul holds numerous instructor certifications in multiple disciplines; nonetheless, he is and will remain a dedicated Student of the Gun.

Zachary shoots while dad coaches at 4H event.

Additional Books by Paul G. Markel

Student of the Gun:

    a Beginner Once, a Student for Life.

Patriot Fire Team:

    Preserving the Republic Four Men at a Time

Faith and the Patriot: A Belief worth Fighting For

All books are available on Amazon.com

Also, follow us at:

www.StudentoftheGun.com

www.StudentoftheGunRadio.com

www.PatriotFireTeam.com

Made in the USA
San Bernardino, CA
29 September 2017